Presenting

Category: Business & Economics
© Copyright: 2017 by Bob Oros Publishing
Standard Copyright License
Author: Bob Oros
ISBN 978-1-105-22296-2
Description: Give reasons why they should buy. Your sales calls will be so much more than just a visit to get an order. You will learn to spend time carefully reviewing the customer's business and meticulously matching your products to their problems. You will give them a well thought out list of "reasons why" you are the best person to provide the solution to their problem. Benjamin Franklin's 13-week self improvement program will guarantee your success.

Key words: sales presentations, better sales presentations

PRESENTING 1

FOCUSED ON THE WRONG THING 5
MOST POWERFUL CONCEPT 5
POLITICIANS 7
TRAVEL AGENCY 8
INSURANCE COMPANIES 8
LAWYERS 9
CREDIT CARDS 9
LAW ENFORCEMENT 10
CONTROL OVER THE INTERVIEW 10
PREPARE THE CUSTOMER 14
DESIGN YOUR PRESENTATION 17
WHAT DOES YOUR PRICE TELL YOUR CUSTOMER? 22
NEVER EXAGGERATE 23
PRESENTING VALUE VS. PRICE 26
JUSTIFY YOUR PRICES 30
PRESENTATIONS: GIVE REASONS WHY THEY SHOULD BUY 33
MY 4% IMPROVEMENT OBJECTIVE: 34
WHAT THIS ENTIRE BOOK SERIES WILL DO FOR YOU 35
ABOUT THE AUTHOR BOB OROS 36
INTRODUCTION TO BEN FRANKLIN'S SYSTEM 37
ACHIEVE A 52% IMPROVEMENT 40

Focused on the wrong thing

Why are most sales presentations focused on the wrong thing? Mainly because we are under the assumption that to sell we have to find the needs of our customer and then work up a presentation that will demonstrate how we can help fill those needs. Here is the problem with finding needs; we are looking for something that does not exist. No one really needs anything. I am sure you have everything you need to get buy, just as our customers do. As a matter of fact if you took away twenty five percent of your competition, effective next Monday morning, how long would it take to fill the needs of their customers? Not long, probably a couple of weeks. It would be an exciting couple of weeks if we call on customers and asked them if they need anything and they actually said yes!

Most powerful concept

Everyone in sales has been searching for a key which would magically unlock the door of the mind of every prospect we call on.

Here it is:

You and I, and every person we know, live in a tomorrow! That tomorrow may be a few hours off. It may be this afternoon or next week, a month, a year, or even ten years from now. Ninety percent of the excitement in the present is the imaginary picture we are constantly recreating in our minds of a tomorrow. It will always be a better tomorrow. We picture ourselves as happier then. We will be healthier, more comfortable, with less worries, with more leisure, with more money, with greater power... we will strangely be freed of the realities that make today far from satisfactory.

This attitude forms the texture of desire. It is at the base of the mind of every person who has lived in America for more than twenty four hours. It is our national philosophy, our habitual trend of thought. We know we are going to be better off tomorrow than we are today. Every waking hour our mind glides out of the present into the future, and we see ourselves as we will be tomorrow.

The business owner never likes the profit and loss statement of today... but tomorrow profits are going to climb! He or she pictures a new line of merchandise or menu item moving quickly at a greater profit.

Today the manager must work three nights a week to keep his or her desk clean, but they picture a tomorrow when this new computer will clean the desk at five o'clock, unfatigued and with peace of mind. Tomorrow! We live most of it today. It is so much better than today. The person who sits across from you now is not thinking about themselves as they are now . . . they are building a mental picture of themselves as they will be tomorrow and tomorrow and tomorrow . . . with this or that added, which they are about to purchase ... which when acquired will make them much happier. They see themselves with more customers, with larger gross profits, lower labor costs and fewer taxes to pay.

Politicians

Successful politicians use this concept in every speech. They know that if they want to stay in office or be elected to office they have to know what the people want and build it in to every talk they give. They never like to talk about the past and very rarely address issues in the present, it's always the future. "I am your bridge to the 21st century". "Your door to the future".

Travel agency

A travel agency always gives you a clear vision of where you are going, never on the trip getting there. A seven day cruise sales presentation shows you the fun you will have on board ship, all the food and entertainment you will enjoy. However, they neglect to tell you about the 7 hour flight to Puerto Rico where you meet the ship and the 4 hours you have to stand on the dock waiting in line.

Insurance companies

The insurance industries entire existence relies on selling you the future. When you buy insurance you spend thousands of dollars and have nothing in return except a piece of paper. They present you with a mental picture of what would happen to your family if you were to die. They show you how many people reach old age without any money or retirement. They give examples of the high cost of going to the hospital for surgery. The insurance companies are experts at getting a piece of your future.   This does not mean that it is good or bad, it simply is the way they sell their products and services.

Lawyers

A good lawyer is the true artist in the area of painting future pictures. They usually do it based on fear of loss. When you tell them about your concern they paint a picture of gloom by blowing your problem up to the maximum. Then, of course, they tell you how much work it would be to take care of it and, with no guarantees, will represent you for a fee.

Credit cards

One of the single largest goals of most people today is to have the money to pay off their credit card balances. How did so many people get in this situation where the average married couple owes around $25,000 in credit card bills? Once we look at the concept of appealing to someone's future, creating impatience and a willingness to go in debt for things they didn't think they could live without, it is easy to understand why people borrow on their future. During the last 12 months over one million people filed personal bankruptcy to get out from under their debts.

Law enforcement

Law enforcement is similar to the way the lawyers use this powerful concept. The worst thing that could happen to an individual is to have their future taken away from them. Every time we watch a movie where someone is put behind bars with no hope we can't help wonder how that would feel. If "would be" criminals new for a fact that they would be caught there would be no crime. What a criminal sees is getting away with something unearned. Getting caught is hardly a possibility for them.

Control over the interview

How would you like to walk into a customer's office and have a powerful tool that will give you complete control over the conversation?

You can do it. Here's how.

Before you go in to see the customer carefully list five things you want to discuss. When you are in the buyers office place this list where the buyer can easily see it.

Without saying a word you have just taken control.

Every buyer or customer works from a list. When you place this list in front of them they will have an IRRESISTIBLE urge to work the list and check each item off. If you don't think the buyer will give you the amount of time to cover every thing you want to talk about you can solve that problem by simply using a yellow pad and a black marker.

I discovered this by accident when I was going to call on an important account and did not have the time to prepare in advance. I took out a yellow pad and made a list of five things I wanted to talk about. When I sat down in the buyer's office I set the pad on the desk where the buyer could see it. I then started talking about point number one on my list.

The conversation started to get side tracked when the buyer was interrupted by a phone call. He hung up the phone, his eyes went to my list and he started talking about point number two.

His secretary entered the room and asked him to step out for a minute. When he returned his eyes again went to the list and we began discussing point number three and then four and five.

The amazing part about this is that he never became impatient with our meeting. He seemed to know that when we completed the five points I had listed on the yellow pad were all discussed we would be finished with our meeting. There were even other sales people waiting to see him and we went over my appointment time by 25 minutes.

This is similar to the law of incomplete information. For some reason you mind cannot stand an unsolved piece of information, or incomplete puzzles. The next time you are watching the evening news watch how they reel you in just before a commercial break.

"Right after this important message from our sponsor we will show you how little Jonnie was able to escape from the burning house without a scratch."

If you are like most folks, you will sit there through the commercials to find out what happened and how he did it. Ant the list seems to work the same way. Your customer has to complete the list - it is how they think.

Two parts to every presentation

1 What does my customer or prospect want?

This is the secret of a "Cutting Edge" sales person. Your average sales person talks about the price, the competition or the product, always in the present tense. The "Cutting Edge" sales person looks at their product or service from a different view point. The first question we should ask when putting together our sales strategy is: What does my prospect or customer want? What are the pictures they have of their future? What are their goals? Where do they want to be next year, the year after, and five years from now? We have to go beyond the money and find out what they are going to do with it once they have it. Once we get this information we can move on to the next step in building our sales presentation.

2 How can the benefits of my products and services enhance my client's future?

When we begin to think in these terms we have crossed the bridge from sales person to a true "Cutting Edge Sales Person". Once we begin to think in these terms, our prospects turn into customers and our customers turn into clients. We have set ourselves apart from the average "peddler" who merely has a sales pitch, and put ourselves in the position of a partner who is working for the same goals and objectives as our client. They will know that you "understand where they are coming from". They will know that you understand their problems and have an 'insight' into what they are trying to accomplish.

Prepare the customer

Let's look at your presentation as you unfold it step by step, from another angle, that part which should come first. A presentation is like any good show. The opening of the first act must be unusually good or your audience will walk out before you get underway. And the first few lines of any play are used by the writer to prepare the way for the action which follows. Therefore the first few words should fit the prospect with a pair of "spectacles" so that he will see what you later display. You might say, for example, "Now I am going to show you the new marketing program which will begin next month". Before I take it out of my brief case I want you to bear in mind that a good marketing plan is one which moves, which has brilliant color, which carries a headline to stop the customer." Then when you bring out your new program, you force him to see it through "spectacles" of your own making, enhancing its value to him.

Never dump a sample, or a prospectus, into his or her lap without first preparing his mind to see what it is. Even a monthly flier should not be shown without first holding it back for a moment until you explain what you are going to show. This move brings into play one of the strongest of his mental attributes ...Curiosity.

Your presentation should be looked upon as a good teaching job. Keep technical terms and discussions out. Don't describe how it is made, what it is made of, what its construction advantages are over a competitor's... unless you do so in terms of what these advantages will mean to the buyer when he uses it. You cannot transport the prospect to this better tomorrow until he or she understands what you are selling. Hence the next step in your presentation is a straight forward teaching job, simply one of downright instruction which must be finished before you can talk about the value of your merchandise.

In going through a prospect's ear to the seat of his imagination in order to help him "take off" to an ideal "tomorrow", you should use all of the known principles of effective speech. Keep the voice low, modulated, which conveys the impression of reserve power and gives casual emphasis to important points when you raise your voice.

The finest check you can use to avoid making this common mistake is to keep in mind constantly your objective, to build a picture of the prospect - seeing him or her using your product. No one is interested in the exact mixture of a product, or the percentage of this or that ingredient, unless they view it from the standpoint of how it will be a benefit, making more money and bringing in more customers.

Here is a good example: I got on the plane and just as I settled in, the woman next to me asked where I was from. I told her, trying not to encourage a conversation.

She not only told me where she was from, she volunteered that she had brain surgery – twice! I tried to look interested but I was tired. She kept going on and on and the next thing I knew, I fell asleep while she was talking.

It was a good reminder on how our customers feel most of the time. Sales people call on their customers and talk about their "brain surgery" while the customer has a hundred things on their mind and a hundred things to do.

What is the solution? How do we get our customers to listen?

Pinpoint relevancy: asking well thought out questions to find out what future pictures your customer has in their mind, and then positioning your product or service with surgical precision to help turn those pictures into reality.

Selling isn't brain surgery, or is it? Selling is psychological brain surgery and pinpoint relevancy is when the sales person asks specific questions about what the prospect is interested in.

If the woman sitting next to me on the plane would have asked me a few questions and used my answers to set the stage for her "brain surgery," I would have felt more engaged and would not have fallen asleep.

However, "where are you from let me tell you about my double brain surgery" just didn't cut it.

The key lesson is simple - engage and set the stage before you tell your story.

Design your presentation

Before making a presentation ask yourself the following questions:

1. Do you have a price advantage or a price problem?

If you do not have an advantageous price, don't say a thing about price. Make sure that your benefits are strong enough to get people interested so that when you follow up directly they will be sufficiently interested to pay a higher price.

2. Who is the person who will buy your product or service?

There's no substitute for actually talking with prospects and customers to see what motivates them to buy your products or those of your competitors. Every situation is different, and you can make the most of your selling and marketing efforts if you make your presentation to the person that can be most influential in the sale.

3. What are the economic benefits of using your product?

If you can say that your product or service will save the customer money, time, or effort, you have a great competitive advantage. If you can document this with figures you'll have a very persuasive story to tell. Don't be afraid to go into the details. If your customer is even the least bit cost conscious, they will listen to every word of your presentation.

4. What is the product made of or what does the service consist of?

Carefully study the product or service you are going to sell. If it is a product, get all the details on how it is made, what it is made of, etc. If it is a service, describe exactly what the service consists of. Write out the description as if you were explaining it to a young child who knew absolutely nothing about it.

5. What does the product or service do best?

All products have several features and benefits that will appeal to prospects. Before you say a word, determine which of the benefits will be most important to the largest segment of your market. Keep in mind that a feature is a fact about the product or service and a benefit is what the feature will do for the customer. People buy benefits, not features.

6. How important are your competitive differences?

Your product or service may be better than that of a competitor on a point that doesn't make any real difference to the person who must make the choice. Don't be fooled into using this advantage as a benefit. Even if you do have a great competitive advantage over other products, never knock the competitors. But do make sure that your reader knows the difference and appreciates what it will mean if your product is bought.

How do you set your price? You may have little choice. If your market facts tell you that all your competitors are selling the same item at one dollar, and if one dollar is the absolute least you can charge and still survive, then the decision makes itself. This, however, is rare; you usually have some flexibility.

Your price (less costs) sets your gross profit--at least on that one sale. Very few businesses, of course, can survive on just one sale. So your gross profit, in actuality, is based on your price, multiplied by your number of units of sale, minus your costs.

Some customers buy on price alone, or with price as a key factor. A very few ignore price completely. Most seek the greatest value, real or imagined, per dollar. This factor is usually known as "perceived value." The "ceiling" and the "floor" are terms that describe the highest and lowest possible price decisions you can make. Your ceiling might be what your competition is offering; your floor might be the lowest price you can charge and still turn a profit.

Sometimes, you may wish, briefly, to sell near or below your cost, in order to get customers to try your product or service. Eventually, of course, you must sell above your cost in order to build gross profit--that is, the dollars that allow you to keep your business in operation.

If you are more efficient than your competitor, you might sell below their price and still generate enough income to pay all your other costs and still end up with a net (or bottom line) profit. If you do sell below your competitor's price, you will probably aim to sell enough extra units to make up for the lost income from lower price. Your gross will very likely be lower than the competitor's on each individual sale. By the same token, higher real or perceived value can let you sell above your competition's price. This can cut your number of units sold just as a lower price raised them. However, if you can compensate for the reduction by the extra dollars you will see with a higher price, income goes up.

Pricing should be a window, not a barrier. For instance, volume discounts to key larger customers usually increase your efficiency and profitability, and thus represent a reasonable basis for a price reduction.

Clearly, your decision can be a little tricky. Your price should probably be somewhere between your cost and your competitor's price. If you decide to charge more than a competitor, you need to have reasons that justify the higher price and/or a superior product or service.

What does your price tell your customer?

With effective, intelligent pricing, you can out-maneuver, out-market, and out-sell your competitor and get a bigger share of the market.

1. More products fail because of a price that is too low, than because of a price that is too high.

2. It is easier to cut prices than raise them.

3. "Prestige" pricing can often build your perceived value.

4. One particularly effective strategy is to start out with a relatively high "prestige" price, then cut the price later. The result is a high perceived level of quality, plus a "value" look.

5. A low (or "defensive") price can discourage new competitors.

6. Price testing with a sample group of customers is an excellent way to get important information. Check for positive or negative reactions at various price levels.

7. Price in such a way that you build up your bottom line.

8. Do not get involved in price conspiracy or price fixing agreements.

9. Your pricing strategy should attract customers and confuse competitors.

Price is a vitally important element in your market strategy. You can usually change it quickly, unlike your product or its packaging.

Never exaggerate

I always encourage sales people to ask for a discount when buying something to see how the person reacts to your request. However, there are a few exceptions.

I was recently in Toledo and a sales person told me about a friend of his who sells parachutes! He said BUYERS ASK FOR A DISCOUNT! I would not advise asking for a discount.

In certain cases you might want to pay a little extra. Open heart surgery. A root canal. In these cases you might want to have them give you some proof of their promised results.

Don't let them make the mistake that many sales people make. This huge mistake is exaggerating. When you are selling an idea or trying to convince someone of something, you more than likely over exaggerate your claims.

To get your idea across you may feel you have to use such overworked phrases as:

"We are number one..."

"We are the best in the business..."

"You can save big money with us..."

As soon as one of these statements are made a red flag goes up in the buyers mind. In your opening statement you have just "unsold" yourself. The buyer, customer or person you are trying to convince knows immediately that you are stretching the truth. The buyer (I refer to anyone you are trying to get to buy into your idea, product or service as a "buyer") has three questions:

1. "So what?"

2. "What's in it for me?"

3. "Can you prove it?"

Instead of using the above overworked phrases you should use facts, figures, and examples in your presentation to justify your statements. These facts make the buyer willing to accept you and your offer. Your goal is to weave the facts into the conversation that makes the buyer understand the LIGITIMACY of what you are saying.

Like a shrewd attorney, you want to present your facts in the strongest possible light. For example: "Our program will increase your profits by 6% - here is how." Or "This product line will cut your labor cost by 3% - I have the facts right here to prove what I am saying." Or "This new marketing system will increase your sales by at least 5% - let me show you what I mean"

An idea is sold not necessarily when you go into your close, but when the buyer agrees with your statements - and that is what you are looking for - buyer commitment.

Your goal is to weave the facts into the conversation that makes the buyer understand the LIGITIMACY of what you are saying.

Presenting value vs. price

I am going to make this crystal clear. When you finish reading this you should easily be able to switch your customer from buying on price to buying on value.

Here are some examples that should shift your thinking and show you how to shift the thinking of your customer.

If you have $100 to spend on dinner to celebrate your kids birthday, what are you going to look for? The best value for your money.

If you have $400 in your budget for a monthly car payment, what are you going to look for? The most car for your payment.

If you have been pre-qualified by the bank to buy a $150,000 house, what are you going to look for? The most house for your money.

If you have 4 kids and a grocery budget of $250 a week, what are you going to look for? The most value for your money.

If you have decided that you are going to spend $2,000 on a new flat screen TV, what are you going to look for? The most TV for your $2,000.

OK, I know what you are thinking. How can you use this to make the sale instead of cutting the price?

Here is how to make the shift in thinking.

You're selling to a restaurant owner. Here is what you say: "You are spending $5,000 per week for your food, so your goal is to get the most value and the highest quality for your $5,000 weekly investment, is that correct? That is why we don't simply throw out prices and try to beat everyone. We take your budget and give you the highest value for your investment. For example, our service, our quality, our in stock items, etc.

You're selling staffing services. Here is what you say: "You are paying $18.00 per hour for an employee, so your goal is to get the most value for your $18.00 per hour investment, is that correct? That is why we don't simply try to beat everyone's hourly price. We take your budget and give you the highest value for your investment. For example, here are 57 services we can offer that makes us the best value for your money.

You're selling a training and coaching program. Here is what you say: "I am sure you will agree, $200 per month per person is a very reasonable investment for training and coaching, especially with the results you will get? Here is why our program delivers so much more value for your investment than anything else available: You can continue until your sales are up to where they need to be. Plus you can miss a session and easily make it up. Plus we can become your ongoing training partner. Plus our training is very interactive - NOT a lecture series! Plus we address your individual selling roadblocks and find solutions! Plus you can quit anytime if you are not happy and your payments stop! Plus you can start RIGHT NOW - NO WAITING - GET IMMEDIATE RESULTS! Plus you can have confidence in our results because we are experts - all we do is sales training! That is more value than any other program available, especially for the small monthly investment, don't you agree?"

You're selling a house. Here is what you say: "I am sure you will agree, the payment on this house is $1,227 per month including taxes and insurance is a stretch. You may be able to find a house with a smaller payment, but look at this street, look at this neighborhood, look at this back yard, how about this great deck, and this fireplace, and these appliances, and the home owner's warranty, and the association benefits, etc."

You are selling a car. Here is what you say: "What is the payment or price range you are looking for? $400 per month. Then our goal is to find you the best value for your investment, let's start with this one I have right here. It not only has a huge rebate, all the great features, but we have marked it down as well. With all this you are actually getting a $600 per month car for a $400 per month investment."

1. You first ask: "How much are you already spending, or how much are you willing to spend, or how much do you have in your budget?"

2. You then ask: "I assume your goal is to get the most value for your investment, is that correct?

3. Your presentation is helping them make the best decision by showing how much value they will get when they buy from you?

Justify your prices

The purpose of your presentation is to justify your prices before they become an objection.

(1) When your customer trusts and knows what to expect from you, you gain an advantage. Consistent quality, delivery, service, and constant innovation create exceptional value in a sale.

(2) When you can demonstrate that your products are guaranteed to arrive in perfect condition, you increase your value. If your competitor's product has ever arrived dented, dirty, or damaged, you've gained an advantage.

(3) A survey found that when a customer perceives that a company responds instantly to their problem, the customer will do business with that company again 95 percent of the time. It's not product failure that causes problems. Its delays that are costly.

(4) Your product may cost less for operator training, a lower cost to run, and reduced cost to repair than a competitive offering. These savings add value and increase the price you can charge.

(5) Smart customers will select a technically sound company over one that's obsolete or on the brink of failure.

(6) Your customer will pay more to eliminate and avoid headaches. Are you "Easy to do business with"?

(7) Gain an advantage by being an expert on your products. Buyers worry when a company rep doesn't know the product. It gets worse if your customer thinks you may have incorrect information.

(8) When your customer is uncertain of the market, they tend to select the vendor with the best reputation.

Here are some of the things a sales person might say to justify the price:

"Yes, our price is higher-but our product has longer shelf life. You will never lose any money because of spoilage. We get it in and out of our warehouse and onto your shelf faster than any other distributor."

Then show him the comparative figures on spoilage. Highlight this benefit he can't get anywhere else.

Presentations:
Give reasons why they should buy

My sales calls are so much more than just a visit to get an order. I spend time carefully reviewing the customer's business and meticulously match my products to their problems. I give them a well thought out list of "reasons why" I am the best person to provide the solution to their problem. I have put so much work into preparing my presentation that I can recite it frontwards and backwards. I have studied all the features and benefits of my products as well as everything my company can do to make it easy for the customer to make a well educated decision to buy from me. When it comes to making a presentation there is no one better sold on my company and my products and services than I am.

My 4% improvement objective:

_____

_____

_____

_____

_____

_____

What this entire Book series will do for you

Buying all 13 books is like buying a library of 13 powerful coaching sessions that will increase every skill necessary for generating business. Once you experience the seemingly effortless improvement you will understand why there is a picture of Ben Franklin on every 100 dollar bill.

You will learn how to improve relationships, improve management skills, be more productive, generate more customers, negotiate better contracts, open new accounts, earn more profits and create more sales! Results most people only dream about! If you are a sales professional or an entrepreneur this is the perfect program to boost your sales and increase your profits.

About the author Bob Oros

The principles in the book series were uncovered the old fashioned way: Hard work. Personal interviews with 507 professional buyers and 3,759 company owners were conducted to uncover the REASONS WHY they bought from certain sales people, or what they did to get a sales person to lower their prices. The information was then tested online by 4,838 new and veteran sales people from all 50 states and six continents to prove these findings would produce results. Since then the principles have been presented in seminars and workshops more than 2000 times for some of the largest companies in the country.

Introduction to Ben Franklin's system

In our fast paced business and personal life today it has become increasingly difficult to set aside time for self development and improving your skills. With every spare minute taken up by reading blogs, logging on to Facebook, following people on Twitter, responding to text messages and emails and constantly talking on your cell phone, there seems to be little, if any, time left for learning new skills. Even the quiet time behind the wheel of your car is no longer available with satellite radio and cell phone coverage in every corner of the country.

Even though this seems like a new problem, distractions have been around forever. Two hundred years ago a man by the name of Ben Franklin had the same problem. He concluded that it was not a matter of distractions as much as a matter of focus. He set out to solve the problem and created the most effective system for self improvement ever invented.

Ben Franklin gives credit for all his success and accomplishments to the implementation of this system for the success he sought after. Despite being born into a poor family and only receiving two years of formal schooling, Ben Franklin became a successful printer, scientist, musician, author and one of the founding fathers of the United States. Ben Franklin is considered to have been one of the most persuasive and successful people in the history of the United States. He was a very skilled sales person, marketer, negotiator and copywriter. Skills that every business owner, professional person, manager and marketer should have.

In the year 1723, Ben Franklin, at the age of seventeen, arrived in Philadelphia without a penny to his name. At age 42, he retired, wealthy, the first self made millionaire in the country. Few people, before or since have ever been as successful as Benjamin Franklin. He gave credit for his many inventions and business successes to his system for self improvement he created when he was 20 years old.

The key to Franklin's success was his drive to constantly improve himself and accomplish his ambitions. In order to accomplish his goal, Franklin developed and committed himself to a personal improvement program that consisted of mastering 13 principles.

When he was seventy-nine years old, Benjamin Franklin wrote more about this idea than anything else that ever happened to him in his entire life. He felt that he owed all his success and happiness to this one thing. Franklin wrote: "I hope, therefore, that some of my descendants may follow the example and reap the benefit."

Since success is developed by performing small and seemingly insignificant acts, you can use this method by reading and putting into practice the 13 skills that will guarantee your success in sales with scientific certainty.

This program takes advantage of Franklin's system and applies it to improving your skills as a sales professional. This program will show you how to dominate your market by first dominating yourself. By focusing on the 13 skills that make up a highly effective and successful sales professional. As these skills are improved your results and sales increases will also show a dramatic improvement.

The goal of going through the program the first time is to increase each skill by only four percent. With the accomplishment of this small improvement in each skill or attitude your overall improvement will be 52%. Those are results most people only dream about. However, you can accomplish this by investing as little as 45 minutes once a week reading one book and then focusing on improving the single skill during the rest of the week. The second week by reading the second book and focusing on that single skill during the week and so on until all 13 weeks are completed.

You can write the single word on the back of your business card and tape it to your dash board as a reminder. You can put this one word on your smart phone as a reminder as well as on your email signature, your Facebook page or you can even have something worthwhile to tweet about. One word, one week, one skill, one "I am" statement, 4% improvement objective and your subconscious mind will receive the message through all the clutter and act on it.

After the first time through the process you can do as Ben Franklin suggests and go through the program a second, third and fourth time. Get your whole sales team on the same page at the same time and you will experience a whirlwind of new excitement and new business. Or get a like minded colleague and join forces with accountability and focus.

Achieve a 52% improvement

Using Franklin's scientific program for learning your objective is to improve 4% in each area over 13 weeks.

1 Planning: To get big results set big goals
2 Questions: Ask questions that make the sale
3 Attention: Get attention with an irresistible offer
4 Presentation: Give reasons why they should buy
5 Objections: Remove every roadblock to the sale
6 Closing: Ask for the order and get paid
7 Follow up: Remove all hope for competitors
8 Attitude: Define what you want and go after it
9 Respect: Earn respect by being an expert
10 Service: Help customers build their business
11 Urgency: Be enthusiastic get things done now
12 Confidence: Remove restrictions and limitations
13 Persistence: Keep going and never give up

For more information visit www.BobOros.com

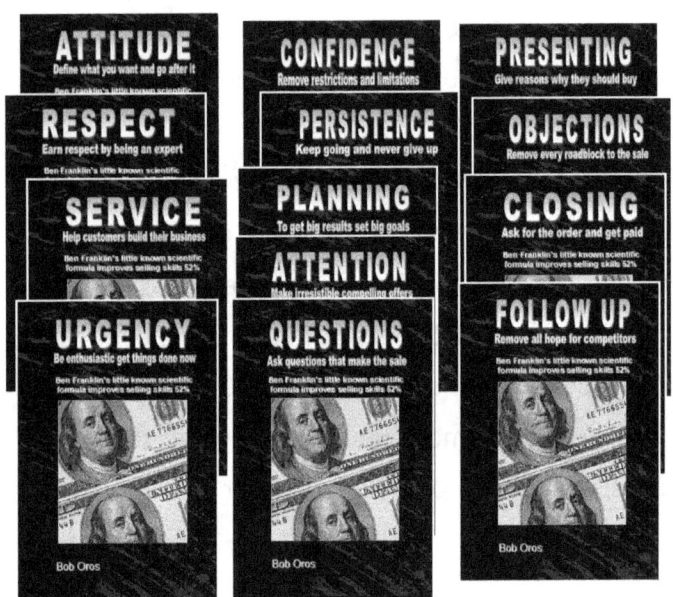

www.ingramcontent.com/pod-product-compliance
Lightning Source LLC
Chambersburg PA
CBHW070433180526
45158CB00017B/1157